Thomas Haupt

Cockatiels

Photographs: Karin Skogstad
Illustrations: György Jankovics
Translated from the German by Rita Kimber

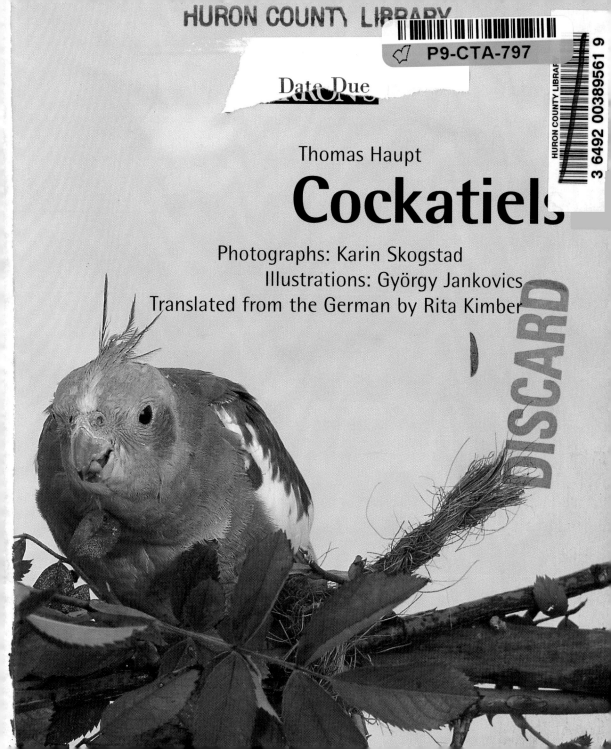

CONTENTS

THE TYPICAL
COCKATIEL

- Pointed crest a striking feature
- Gets along with others of its kind
- Friendly disposition; enjoys human company
- Black button eyes and delicate colors
- Enterprising and curious
- Slender shape
- Young stay in the nest until they fledge
- Easy to keep and to breed
- Loud voice that may take time getting used to
- Needs periods of free flying to stay healthy

Its pleasant disposition, the ease with which it reproduces, and its simple requirements in captivity make the cockatiel an ideal "first bird," and it is in fact a favorite among aviculturists. Its adaptability and playfulness make it attractive not only to breeders but also to anyone simply wishing to have a pet bird. Cockatiels can also become good friends of children or companions of people who live alone.

nute Wave of Silence

moving across Car
f it. At 11 a.m. ir
o stand silently,
ir futures so t
friends and

DECISION MAKING

1 Cockatiels can live as long as 15 or 20 years. Are you ready to commit yourself for such a long time?

2 Bird cages and indoor aviaries are not cheap. Can you afford the purchase price and, more important, the ongoing costs for upkeep?

3 Cages have to be kept clean, food and water changed daily. Do you have time for these daily chores?

4 Cockatiels are sociable birds that live in flocks. Will you be able to satisfy your bird's need for daily contact and play?

5 When your bird flies free in your home it may deposit droppings and chew on furniture and wooden objects. Can you put up with this?

6 Even though a cockatiel is a suitable pet for teaching children a sense of responsibility, an adult still has to check daily that the bird is properly cared for.

7 Do you have a place to take the bird to or a caretaker to look after it when you go away on vacation?

8 When your bird gets sick you may have to take it to the veterinarian. Can your budget absorb extra costs for veterinarian's bills and medicines?

9 Do you already have pets that would not get along with a bird?

10 Is there a family member or anyone else living in your household who is allergic to feather dust, is bothered by noise, or doesn't like animals?

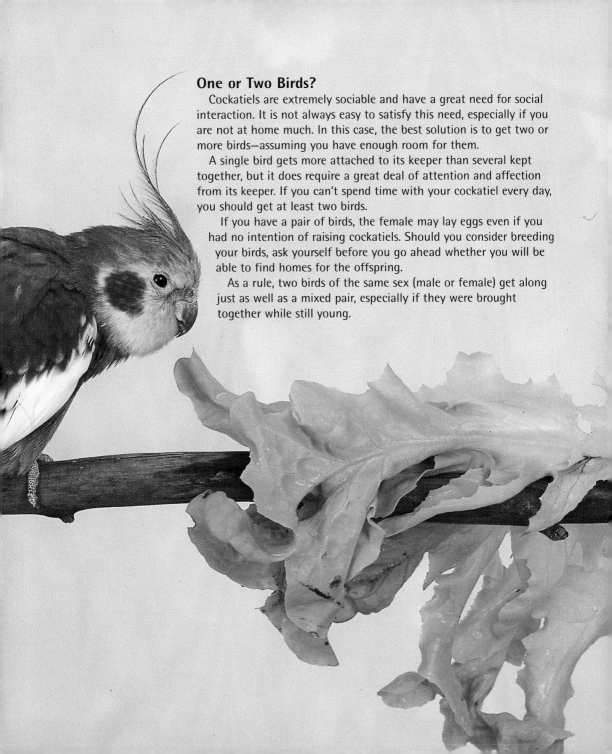

One or Two Birds?

Cockatiels are extremely sociable and have a great need for social interaction. It is not always easy to satisfy this need, especially if you are not at home much. In this case, the best solution is to get two or more birds—assuming you have enough room for them.

A single bird gets more attached to its keeper than several kept together, but it does require a great deal of attention and affection from its keeper. If you can't spend time with your cockatiel every day, you should get at least two birds.

If you have a pair of birds, the female may lay eggs even if you had no intention of raising cockatiels. Should you consider breeding your birds, ask yourself before you go ahead whether you will be able to find homes for the offspring.

As a rule, two birds of the same sex (male or female) get along just as well as a mixed pair, especially if they were brought together while still young.

PREPARATION AND PURCHASE

With its tufted crest and black button eyes, a cockatiel is an impish looking little bird that quickly charms its owners with its bright and cheerful ways. But for the bird to be happy in your home, certain criteria have to be met.

Origin

Cockatiels come from Australia, where they prefer open spaces, preferably near water. They are often found in areas where grain is grown. They live in pairs or small flocks, though when migrating or at water holes, up to 1,000 birds may come together.

When ranging across the continent in search of food, the birds depend on their excellent flying skills and endurance. They travel straight and fast, constantly utter loud cries while in the air to maintain contact, and land only to eat and drink. When on the ground they are very shy because of the danger of predators.

Cockatiels feed on the seeds of grasses and weeds, as well as on fruit and grain. If a flock alights on a wheat field, it may cause much damage, and farmers are, therefore, not very fond of the birds.

In Australia, cockatiels generally breed between August and December. Mating is triggered by the presence of sufficient food and water. As cavity breeders, cockatiels build their nests in holes in old trees. Cockatiels do not display strict territorial behavior but defend only the immediate entry to their nest cavity against others of their kind. Consequently, several pairs can breed one above the other in cavities of the same tree.

Cockatiels are playful rascals. Appropriate toys keep them from getting bored.

Cockatiels as Pets

Nymphicus hollandicus—that's the cockatiel's scientific name—was first brought to Europe around 1840. In the early years collectors took young birds from their nests or caught entire flocks in order to satisfy the demand of zoos and bird fanciers for this parrot species. But on the long journey by boat, a great many birds perished and people began to breed them in Europe.

Cockatiels were first successfully bred in Europe around 1850. Once the initial problem of providing appropriate nest sites was solved, breeding the birds became relatively easy. This was a good thing because in 1894 the Australian government imposed an export embargo on all native cockatiels. Today, the species is considered domesticated and is not subject to any regulations of species protection.

Where to Buy Cockatiels

Cockatiels are sold at pet stores, where you can usually choose from among a number of birds with different coloration (see page 12). You can also buy cockatiels from a serious breeder. You can get information on breeders from bird clubs or animal shelters. Any reputable pet dealer or responsible breeder will be knowledgeable and will try to offer only healthy birds in good condition. You should definitely buy a young bird if you expect it to become tame.

I strongly advise against buying cockatiels by mail. The stress of the journey leaves the birds weakened and susceptible to disease. Besides, you have no opportunity to observe the bird or its companions in the cage before you buy it.

Things to Consider

Take plenty of time when buying your cockatiel and observe the various birds for sale carefully. Talk to the salesperson or breeder.

What you should watch for:
✔ If any birds exhibit signs of sickness, if their plumage is ruffled, or they sit apathetically in a corner, you should not buy them. The danger of acquiring a sick bird is too great.

Agile gymnasts, cockatiels make use of any opportunity to climb.

✔ Make sure everything is calm and quiet while you select your bird. Cockatiels are flock animals. If there is noise or a bustle in the room, all the birds, including the sick ones, will sit with their plumage pressed flat against the body so as not to reveal anything about their state to a possible enemy.

✔ All parrot species molt gradually. This means that the plumage is always complete and should be sleek, except when the birds are sleeping, in which case the feathers may be slightly puffed out. Sellers sometimes say that birds with bald spots or damaged plumage are molting, but in most cases these birds are sick.

✔ All parts that do not grow feathers—that is, beak, feet, and cloaca—should be smooth and without welts (danger of burrowing mites, see page 53).

✔ The cages in which the birds for sale are kept should be large enough to accommodate the birds, clean, and with plenty of light.

✔ Do the birds have enough fresh food and water?

✔ Is there a layer of sand at the bottom of each cage?

✔ Watch the behavior of the birds. Are most of them sleeping? Are some of them very puffed up? Is the cage overcrowded?

✔ Do the birds have the possibility to satisfy, at least partially, their need for exercise and for flying, and do they make use of the opportunity?

All these observations and questions are important in helping you decide whether or not to purchase a particular bird. If the pet store or breeder or the birds or their quarters seem questionable to you, don't buy in that establishment, not even out of pity. Life with a new member in your household should not start with a visit to the veterinarian. No serious and reasonable dealer or breeder will try to talk you into buying.

General Nature

Cockatiels can be very deliberate in their ways; they are not usually excitable birds. Their voices can be shrill, but content birds usually use this type of sound only to give out a warning noise when alarmed (or, in males, when performing a display of courtship). More

Cockatiels are happiest when they are with others of their own kind.

often, they use their voices for whistling or for imitating words that they frequently hear.

Cockatiels can become lovable, tame, and trusting companions once they overcome their initial shyness and fear of entering new surroundings. They are usually content as long as they have things to work on with their beaks, such as branches, nibble sticks, or limestone blocks. Once you have the opportunity to observe your birds daily, you will become accustomed to their behavior patterns, their likes and dislikes, and you will see their personalities develop.

TIP

Choosing the Right Cockatiel

Signs that a cockatiel is healthy:
✔ Smooth plumage hugging the body.
✔ No breaks or bald spots in the plumage, even in juveniles. Fledglings leaving the nesting box are always fully feathered unless there is some health problem.
✔ Clear eyes free of discharge.
✔ No discharge from the nose.
✔ The cloaca is clean, without smears of feces.
Signs of illness:
✔ Subdued, apathetic behavior.
✔ Ruffled and disorderly plumage.
✔ Diarrhea.
✔ Sticky eyelids.
Never buy a cockatiel from a cage where there are sick birds because the infection may have spread to all the birds.

Male or Female?

If you want a cockatiel simply because you enjoy birds, the sex of the animal is not very important. Male and female birds become equally tame if you acquire them while they are young.

But if you care about the bird's ability to mimic and sing, you should get a cock, as the male birds are called. As part of their courtship behavior, with which they woo the chosen female, males often mimic sounds they hear. For more on the mimicking talent of cockatiels, see page 51.

If you intend to breed the birds, you obviously have to know their gender. Sexing cockatiels is difficult only in the case of juveniles,

when males and females look almost identical. In older birds and those with the coloring of wild cockatiels, the sexes can be told apart most easily by the shade of the mask, the area of the face that in males is set off conspicuously from the rest of the plumage. The mask of older males is yellow, that of females, pale yellow with a hint of gray. In juveniles the mask is still very muted. Both sexes have a red cheek spot, but in older males the red is brighter. Juveniles don't develop their facial coloring until they are eight or nine months old. Another difference is that in females the tail has horizontal yellow and black barring and the edges of the tail feathers are whitish; in males these feathers are gray.

If you are not sure about the sex of the bird you'd like to buy, ask the pet dealer or breeder.

Color Variants

In the course of captive breeding, cockatiels have been created in various colors that differ more or less markedly from those of the wild birds. Color mutations also occur in nature, but the oddly colored birds rarely survive and have little chance to pass on their genes. The situation is different in captivity. Here the breeder can select specific birds to bring out or eliminate certain traits in the offspring. When you buy a cockatiel, choose whatever color appeals to you. Color is no indication of a bird's character, talent, or disposition. The only thing to consider is that the sexes are harder to tell apart in some color strains than in others.

The following are the most common colors:
Wild-type: These birds are mostly gray. The breast and abdomen may be paler, and some individuals have a brownish tint. The crest and the mask (forehead and face) of the male are a bright yellow; in the female the mask is grayish. Both sexes have orange cheek or ear

spots, which are more brightly colored in the male. The outer tail feathers are yellow in the female but with pronounced dark gray marbling. Young birds resemble the female except that the males have more yellow feathers in the head area. Juveniles acquire their adult plumage at about eight months.

Lutinos: In this type, all pigmentation except yellow is eliminated, and the birds therefore appear yellowish. They are not albinos because some color pigments are left, but, like albinos, these birds have red eyes. The pairing of Lutinos has led to the bald spot on the back of the head typical of this strain, which may be passed on to other color variants. The gene for Lutino coloring is linked to the sex chromosome, which means that these

Fruits and vegetables are essential ingredients of a balanced diet.

hereditary traits show up only in certain birds, depending on the sex of the parent carrying the trait.

Pied: The appearance of this type is quite varied. Pieds have white or yellow patches of various size all over the body. There are also Pieds in different color combinations.

Cinnamons: This type probably originated in Belgium. The gray color of these birds is lighter than that of the Wild-type, and the entire body has a delicate cinnamon hue. The other parts of the plumage are like those of the Wild-type. The nestlings have red eyes, but the eye color changes over time. This color variation, too, is sex-linked.

Pearl: This type was first bred in Germany around 1967. In these birds the feathers on the back, throat, breast, and rump are gray with light edges; or are light colored with dark edges. This gives them a kind of fish-scale appearance. The crest is dark. While young, the males resemble female birds, but as they grow up, the pearled look disappears, and as adults they look like Wild-type cockatiels. Birds whose light-colored feathers are bright yellow are called Golden Pearls.

Silver: This type is a light gray with what looks like a dusting of silver. These birds have red eyes. They are almost indistinguishable from light-colored Wild-type cockatiels.

Caution: Because of a lethal gene, some offspring of two Silver parents die while still in the egg.

White-faced: This type has no yellow or orange whatsoever at any age. The mask of the male, therefore, is pure white. The head of the female is a light gray. Even the down feathers of the nestlings are white. This mutation first appeared in Europe around 1978.

Albinos: This type lacks all pigment and is therefore pure white with red eyes. The beak and claws are also whitish. This variant resulted from the crossing of White-faced and Lutino birds.

Crossing color strains has produced variants such as Cream or Isabel, Whites (which are actually a very pale yellow), yellow birds with black eyes, Cinnamon-Pieds, and Cinnamon White-faced.

P O R T R A I T S :
COCKATIELS

Cockatiels are bred in many different color variations, but there is no connection between the shade of the plumage and a bird's temperament and behavior.

Right: A Wild-type male in full adult plumage.

Left: A Pearled cockatiel contemplating an apple.

Left, below: The Pearled cockatiel is inviting the Pied bird to scratch its neck.

Above: A Lutino busy with a spray of millet.

Below: Two Pieds peacefully eating
spray millet.

Above: A Lutino and a
Pied female fighting
over spray millet.

Left: A
gorgeous
Pied.

Above: A Wild-type at left and
a Pearl at right.

Left: A Lutino at left and a
Wild-type at right.

Legal Questions

If your lease contains no clause concerning pets, you may assume that conventional pets like hamsters, guinea pigs, canaries, and small parrots are allowed. But be considerate of your neighbors—cockatiels can be quite loud. Also remember that as the owner of the bird you are liable for any harm or damage it may cause, as by biting or by chewing on things.

A purchase agreement, which is in writing, is a legal contract. If your cockatiel turns out to be sick or to have some defect when you get it, you may return the bird and are entitled to be reimbursed.

In some states, regulations aimed at preventing the spread of psittacosis, an infectious disease that can also affect humans, require that cockatiels wear identification rings or bands. If a bird comes down with the disease, these rings allow authorities to trace the breeder or aviculturist where the disease originated and to take appropriate measures.

Buyers of parrots are required to leave their name and address at the pet store or breeder's. This information and the ring number of the bird (any one number is issued only once) are entered in that state's official registry and have to be kept.

There are two kinds of rings: The official ring will have a combination of numbers and/or letters on it. It may be open and placed around the leg when the bird is already fairly large. The second kind of ring may be a closed band and is put on while the bird is still nesting. As the bird grows larger, the ring can no longer be removed. These rings might include information such as the hatch year or the state.

Since cockatiels are not among the endangered parrots listed in the Convention on International Trade in Endangered Species (CITES), no papers are required for the purchase or sale of the birds.

Housing and Supplies

You should buy and set up the cage for your cockatiel before you go out to buy the bird.

Size: I can give you only a minimum size. A cage should be no smaller than 24 × 16 × 24 inches (60 × 40 × 60 cm) for a single bird. The rule of thumb is that your bird has to be able to spread out both wings without touching anything and that the tail should not constantly brush against the cage bars. The perches should therefore not be located too close to the side walls. The height of the perches is secondary, but be sure the bird can always sit upright.

Spreading the wings and tail aids relaxation.

Cage decorations are generally of no practical use and just get in the way. Their appeal is limited to the owner; to the cockatiel they serve no purpose.

The floor plan of the cage should be rectangular. Round cages ought to be relegated to museums. Because the bars of round cages are vertical the bird can't make use of them for climbing, and because of their small diameter these cages don't offer enough room for movement.

The cage should have at least two doors, and fairly large ones, so you can clean the cage and perform other necessary chores without having to bend and twist uncomfortably. Even the danger of escape doesn't justify small doors.

The horizontal bars of the cage provide opportunity for climbing.

Clean-out drawers should slide in and out smoothly.

A large cage should be placed on a stand with rollers. This makes maintenance easier and also allows you to move the bird to a window or onto the balcony for a change of scenery. You do, however, have to be careful not to expose the bird to drafts or to direct sunlight that it can't get away from.

Perches

Perches should be thick enough so that the bird's toes can't reach all the way around them.

Preparation and Purchase

Large perches help wear down the claws so that they don't grow too long. Natural sticks and branches are best because their irregularities provide a kind of massage for the feet. The birds also like to nibble on the bark, which supplies them with some minerals and gives them something to do.

Branches of conifers, though not poisonous, are not acceptable because they tend to be very resinous. The resin can get the feathers sticky, and if it gets into the digestive tract it can lead to death.

The right number of perches is also important for the well-being of a cockatiel. If there are too many, they interfere with the bird's movements. The best arrangement is to have one perch in the upper part of the cage, a second one somewhat lower, and a third one still a little higher.

The space between the perches should be large enough so that the bird's tail doesn't constantly rub against a lower perch. This damages the feathers.

Don't place the perches too low. Birds like to sit high up in order to have a good view of their surroundings. The only low perches should be in front of the food dishes.

Food tastes best if it's shared with a friend.

Food Dishes

Get at least three dishes: one for dry food, one for fruit and sprouts, and one for water. The dishes can be of metal, hard plastic, or china. What is important is that they be the right size and easy to clean. It is essential to check and replenish food and water dishes daily.

Automatic food dispensers are not recommended for cockatiels because they can get clogged. They give the false sense that the bird has plenty of food when it may in fact be unable to get at fresh seeds.

Bird Grit

Birds have to have grit in order to get the minerals they need in sufficient quantity. Grit is spread on the bottom of the cage, and some should always be available in a special separate dish as well.

Pet stores sell a special sandpaper for the cage floor, but this paper doesn't supply adequate amounts of sand, and it also hurts the skin on the birds' feet. The same holds for sandpaper sold to be put on the perches to help wear down the claws. The damage caused clearly outweighs the slight good the paper may do. If you use newspaper as a floor covering, make sure the bird doesn't ingest too much of it.

Toys

Give your cockatiel unbreakable objects made of metal or hardwood to play with.

Toys made of sisal are dangerous because the bird may get entangled in the fibers, or if some of the sisal is eaten, the bird may develop inflammation of the crop or digestive problems (see page 54).

Important: Even if your cockatiel has a large and well laid-out cage, your bird must be able to spend some time outside of it. Cockatiels are strong and agile flyers and need lots of exercise, which they can get only if they can fly free (see page 23).

Placement of the Cage

When your bird first arrives in its new home, the cage or indoor aviary should already be placed where it is going to stay permanently.

✔ The cage should be near a window. This way the bird can watch what is going on outside, it is exposed to the natural rhythm of day and night, and it gets a chance to get some sun. However, the bird must always be able to retreat to the shade.

✔ The cage should not be too low because birds must be able to survey the world around them. Eye level with people is about the right height.

✔ Put the cage where you spend much of your time; otherwise, the bird will be lonely and will fail to get attached to you.

✔ There should be no heater or radiator nearby. Rising hot air dries out a bird's mucous membranes and can lead to illness.

✔ Smoke is harmful to birds.

Checklist
Cage and Equipment

1 Metal cage with sufficiently large doors, an unbreakable bath, and a clean-out drawer.

2 If you are buying only one cockatiel but are considering adding another, the cage should be no smaller than 40 × 28 × 51 inches (100 × 70 × 130 cm).

3 Cage bars should always be horizontal and spaced $5/8$ to $3/4$ of an inch (1.5 to 2 cm) apart.

4 Perches of hardwood dowels or branches of unsprayed fruit trees, shrubs, willows, poplars, or nut trees.

5 At least three food dishes of metal, hard plastic, or china, for water, dry food, and fruit and sprouts.

6 Unbreakable toys made of metal or hardwood.

7 Bird grit for the cage bottom and as an aid to digestion.

8 A spray bottle to give the cockatiel showers (see page 34).

The Trip Home

You will be handed your cockatiel in a travel box especially designed so that the bird will not hurt itself and will stay calm. This box will later come in handy for trips to the veterinarian. Take the bird home without making stops along the way. When you get there, hold the open box up to the cage, which you will have prepared for its occupant beforehand, and wait until the cockatiel climbs through the cage door. You

This cockatiel is obviously happy to be near a window.

may have to wait several minutes. Then go away; the bird should not be bothered the first day in its new home.

Winning the Bird's Trust

The first few days are usually the most difficult. Do the necessary caretaking chores quietly and always in the same way. That makes the process less threatening.

If your cockatiel is very shy, sit down at some distance from the cage and talk to the bird in a soft, reassuring tone.

By moving your hand slowly toward the bird's abdomen, you will gradually win your bird's trust.

Hand-taming a Cockatiel

✔ Gradually move closer to the cage when you talk to the bird.
✔ When your cockatiel is accustomed enough to you that you can stand next to the cage, put your hand against the bars, but not above the bird; otherwise, the bird might think a predator is approaching from above.

✔ Slowly reach inside the cage and extend your hand toward the bird.
✔ When your hand is very close to the bird, start stroking its head gently. Offering a treat at the same time may do wonders.
✔ Move your hand to the bird's abdomen from below and push up a little. The bird will often respond by climbing onto your hand.
✔ Practice this until the cockatiel always climbs onto your hand when you encourage it to do so.
✔ Don't take the bird out of the cage until the bird consistently climbs onto your hand. Avoid abrupt movements.

This is how your cockatiel learns to climb onto your finger.

Night Rest

As a rule, cockatiels follow an inborn schedule of rest and wakefulness, which you should respect. But the birds are also flexible and will often adjust to your daily life rhythm. It is important, however, that their night rest be undisturbed.

When a cockatiel gets ready to retire, it settles down on its sleeping perch. At this point it should be left undisturbed. To prevent the bird from waking up at night startled, flying up, and possibly hurting itself,

Undisturbed sleep is important for the bird's health.

you can leave on a small night light (10 or 20 watt).

Don't cover the cage with a cloth. This gives the bird the feeling of being caught under a net.

Minor squabbling over treats is nothing to worry about, but if a real fight develops you have to separate the birds.

Getting Two Birds Used to Each Other

If you already have one cockatiel and then get a second one, or if you have bought two, you should be present for the first few hours the birds spend together in order to prevent fights or accidents. Although cockatiels usually get along well together, problems may arise. The established bird often takes a few days before it accepts the new partner.

If the cage or aviary is quite large, you can place both birds in it and watch them. If there is only minor bickering but no real fighting in the first few hours, things usually continue peacefully. But if the birds attack each other you have to separate them.

Keep the birds in separate cages next to each other. After a while they can be brought together on neutral ground, perhaps in the room. If all goes well, both birds can be put in one cage.

The sex of the two birds is usually not very important. Birds of the same gender often get along as well as a mixed pair.

DAILY MANAGEMENT AND CARE

Once your cockatiel has overcome its fear of you and climbs onto your hand, you will start having a wonderful time with it. But in order to offer it a full and happy life you have to make sure you respect its natural needs, feed it a healthy and varied diet, and take good care of it.

Flying Free

Once your cockatiel hops onto your hand without hesitation you can prepare for the next step, letting it fly free in a room. But don't be in a rush. Give the bird enough time to become very familiar with the room and everything in it from the cage. Since cockatiels are fast flyers, serious accidents can result if a bird is not well enough acquainted with the room. It is important for the bird to assess the space and its limitations accurately. (See page 27 for how to make the room bird-proof.)

The first free flight has to take place under your supervision. Even later you should not let the bird fly free for more than five or ten minutes if you are not there to watch. In my opinion, a cockatiel belongs in its cage when the caretaker is not around. The cage is the safest place for it; nothing can happen to it there and there won't be any occasions later on for you to feel that you were negligent.

The bird should fly free only in the room where it lives. Once it is used to flying free there, you can let it explore other rooms to provide some change in the daily routine, but never forget to take the proper precautions (see page 27).

Don't chase the cockatiel out of its cage for its first flight outside. Either let it take its time to emerge from the cage door or take it out on your hand. In the latter case it will associate the pleasure of flying free with your hand and will be even more eager to hop onto your finger.

To return the bird after its free flying session, proceed the same way. If you are lucky, the bird will get back into the cage on its own because it is hungry or tired. Never try to chase it back or it will have only negative feelings about returning to its cage.

If your bird is used to sitting on your hand, you can place it in the cage that way. If it should try to fly off again, you can restrain it with a finger—but never lose your patience with the bird, no matter what.

Offer food only in the cage or on your hand. This makes the cage a more attractive place to return to.

Landing has to be practiced, just like flying. The first few attempts are usually crash landings, but the bird will soon get more skilled.

Cockatiels like to nibble on plants. Make sure there are no poisonous ones around.

Poisonous and Dangerous Plants

When flying free in a room, cockatiels like to nibble on plants; unfortunately, they cannot tell poisonous from harmless ones. That's why it's up to you to make sure that there are no dangerous plants or substances that could make the bird sick anywhere where the bird might get at them.

House and garden plants considered poisonous:

Euphorbia species, Dieffenbachia, crown-of-thorn, yew, hyacinth, periwinkle, deadly nightshade, poinsettia, narcissus, oleander, Ardisia, four-o'clock, maidenhead fern.

Considered extremely dangerous:

Ivy, philodendron, flamingo flower (*Anthurium*), golden trumpet (*Allamanda cathartica*), resinous woods, *Schefflera*.

With cacti special caution is in order because of their spines. Young birds are especially likely to get hurt because they are still inexperienced and clumsy.

Before buying a new plant, ask if it might be harmful to birds. Better to do without the plant than take a chance with your cockatiel's well-being.

A local garden center, a county extension office, or an avian veterinarian can help determine if specific plants are safe.

This applies especially to juveniles. If a room is large enough for a young bird to develop speed, a disaster may be in the making when the flight is stopped abruptly by a wall or a window. In nature there are no such obstacles. That is why it is important that you always be present during a young bird's first flights.

In time your cockatiel will develop a preference for certain spots. Prepare these spots by placing newspaper under them to catch the droppings. Cockatiels don't usually gnaw much or chew on wood, but you can't assume that they will leave furniture and wallpaper untouched, and that, too, may be a source of danger. Try to distract your bird from unwanted gnawing by setting up fresh branches now and then or by giving it a climbing tree (see page 51). But don't put the tree too close to the cage; you want the bird to fly to it. This way, the bird gets the healthy exercise it needs because it has to fly back and forth when it wants to eat or drink.

If you feel that your house is not safe for a bird to fly in, or you have trouble taming the bird, consider trimming the wing feathers. Trim only the longest feathers on the outside of the wing. Ask a veterinarian how to demonstrate proper trimming of the feathers.

A door is a good vantage point, but toes can get pinched when the door closes.

Avoiding Dangers

Source of Danger	Danger	Avoiding the Danger
Open doors	Flying into rooms not meant for the bird	Keep doors closed to all rooms where bird is not supposed to fly
Open door used by bird as lookout	Feet are caught when door closes	Always check bird's whereabouts
Clothes lying on floor	Bird crawls under them and may get hurt	Get used to walking gingerly; don't leave things lying around
Containers with water	Bird may slip in and drown	Always watch the bird; if necessary, cover container
Open closets and drawers	Bird is closed in by mistake	Always keep closets and drawers closed or check them frequently
Poisons like alcohol, magic markers, salt, verdigris, solvents, fertilizers, cleansers, lead weights in drapes	Poisoning by ingestion	Keep poisonous substances in inaccessible places; don't offer alcohol, even as a joke at parties
Stove burners, hot irons, candles, fireplace, nonstick cooking surfaces	Burns, possibly fatal; poisoning by inhalation	Always keep bird in cage when you cook or iron or have an open fire; avoid airborne toxins
Waste basket, decorative vases	Bird slips in and is unable to climb out again	Woven baskets are easier to climb out of; filling vessels with sand prevents bird from falling in; cover vessels while bird is flying free
Direct sun for prolonged period	Heatstroke and heart attack	Place cage so bird can choose to be in sun or shade
Stoves, electrical appliances	Burns, fatal electric shock if bird chews on wires	Put appliances where bird can't get at them; cover securely
Extreme temperature fluctuations	Colds, pneumonia, heatstroke, freezing to death	Gradually acclimatize bird to changes in temperature

10 Golden Rules
on Proper Care

1 If you want to make sure from the beginning that you'll have a happy bird, get two cockatiels.

2 In all your dealings with the bird, act quietly and calmly; a hectic pace makes any bird nervous.

3 Get the cockatiel used to your hand. Always raise your hand toward its abdomen from below and encourage the bird to step onto it.

4 Never leave children under the age of 12 alone with the bird; this way both parties are safe from accidents.

5 Don't approach your cockatiel unexpectedly with quick movements; this would scare it.

6 Regular free flying and other activities are important; they keep your bird healthy and in good shape, and they provide entertainment.

7 A cockatiel cannot be housebroken. Knowing this, take appropriate measures, such as spreading newspapers on the floor.

8 Rearrange the inside of the cage periodically and offer food in new places. That keeps the bird alert.

9 Variety in the composition of the bird's diet is important; so is a regular feeding schedule, which will help you not to forget anything.

10 Clean the cage and everything in it regularly to prevent disease, but don't use disinfectants; these are generally too strong for birds. Also, the immune system has no chance to function in excessively hygienic surroundings.

A Bird-proof Room

To make sure your bird is safe when flying
you have to take some precautions.

✔ Check that all windows in the room are
completely shut. Your bird would not be the first
to escape through a cracked window. You may
want to put up screens so that fresh air can still
enter the room, which is important for your bird.

✔ Pull the curtains or lower the shades. Birds
don't know about glass and will try to fly
through what looks to them like an opening.
Crashing against a window can cause serious
injury and even death. You can gradually open
the curtains or shades a couple of inches a day,
to get the bird used to the glass.

✔ Bureaus and cupboards have to be shoved up
against the wall so the cockatiel can't slip behind
them and be unable to get out again on its own.

✔ Don't leave filled flower vases or watering
cans standing around; if the cockatiel peers in
to see what's there, it may slip in and drown.

✔ Birds like to chew on electric wires—with
possibly fatal results. If you can, run the wires
behind furniture or under rugs, or run them
through a metal pipe.

✔ Keep no poisonous plants or objects made of
pewter or lead in the room. The bird might
nibble on them. Many substances are toxic for
birds, among them sprays, diuretics, mercury,
plastic film and bags, glues, varnish, spices, and
ballpoint pen cartridges.

What to Do if the Bird Escapes

Cockatiels are swift flyers that can develop
speed even inside a room, so if you don't watch
even for a minute your bird might get away.

Once outside, the cockatiel will quickly fly
high up in the air to orient itself, especially
if there are no trees around. Since the bird
doesn't know the area, it will move farther and
farther away looking for familiar landmarks or

*These two birds are about to enjoy some free
flying.*

its caretaker. This way it can cover considerable
distances, and finding it again is now a matter
of pure luck.

In the summer the bird may survive in the
wild for a time as long as it doesn't fall victim
to a raptor or a cat, fly into a power line, or
get hit by a car. It will find seeds, fruit, and
berries to eat. Not so in winter when it may
manage for a while by joining a flock of wild
birds and visiting bird feeders. The cold is not
that serious, but in the long run a cockatiel will
not survive on its own.

The bird may luck out if hunger or tameness
drives it to seek out people. If that happens,
the ring on its foot makes it possible to find
the rightful owner.

If your cockatiel has escaped but is still close
by, place its cage with food in it outside and

VACATION PLANS

Vacation time raises the question of what to do with the bird.

For two days or less you can leave your cockatiel in its cage with plenty of food and water. This is least stressful for the bird.

If you are going to be away for a longer time, you have to make arrangements ahead of time:

✔ *If you are not going a great distance, you can take your bird along in a smaller travel cage. Don't expose it to drafts, heat, or full sun on the way. Make sure to ask ahead if the bird is welcome where you are going.*

✔ *Find a place where you can board your bird. Ask at your pet store, local animal shelter, or veterinarian. Or perhaps a friend or relative is willing to take in your bird. An even better solution is if the vacation caretaker can stay in your house or apartment and look after the bird in its familiar surroundings.*

✔ *Make preparations for your absence way ahead of time. Write up a sheet with directions, including important addresses and where you can be reached, and leave it with the caretaker.*

hope the bird will find its way back into it. If the bird has settled on a tree that is not too tall, you can aim a strong spray of water at it; a bird can't fly if its plumage is soaked. But you have to do it quickly; if the bird gets scared before it is immobilized, it will disappear for good.

In the wild, cockatiels behave in a way you can make use of when attempting to retrieve your bird. A pair of cockatiels will try to keep in contact with each other by calling constantly if one partner is not close by. Sometimes the bird that stays behind lures its runaway mate back to the cage with its calls.

Cockatiels and Children

Cockatiels are not ideal pets for children, especially for very young ones. They don't like to be petted and cuddled, and children's hands may unintentionally be too rough for the small feathered body.

If your child insists on a bird, keep in mind that a cockatiel needs not only affection but also proper care and things to occupy it. Also remember that keeping a bird costs money, though not vast sums. A child has to be 12 to 15 years old before you can entrust it with the responsibility for a bird. With a younger child you have to take care of the daily chores yourself, or at least check to see that everything gets done. Children often lose interest in a bird rather soon, and then you will have to take over as caretaker.

If your child is truly interested in keeping birds, especially small parrots, a cockatiel is— along with the budgerigar—the most perfect first bird because its care is relatively simple and it becomes tame quite quickly. Thus, a close friendship between child and bird can develop that lasts for years, while the child learns to take responsibility for another creature.

Cockatiels and Other Pets

Generally speaking, cockatiels get along well with just about any birds. You can combine them with other small parrots, like budgerigars, or other kinds of birds, such as canaries or exotic finches. Just make sure the cage or aviary is large enough for the birds to get away from each other and for them to be able to establish small territories for breeding. Set up such a mixed group only when the birds are not in their breeding cycle in order not to jeopardize the success of the mating.

Dogs, unless they have a pronounced hunting instinct, generally show little interest in cockatiels, but you should never leave the two animals alone together, even if you are at home. Big dogs can sometimes seriously hurt a bird without intending to, simply because of their clumsiness.

Cats are more problematic because they are hunters by nature. A relatively peaceful coexistence can be achieved if the cockatiel learns from the beginning to defend itself with its beak whenever the cat gets too close. But this generally works only if the cat is introduced to the bird as a kitten. Even in that case, never leave cat and bird alone together. The cat might pounce during a moment of inattention on the part of the bird.

Always keep in mind that cockatiels are very docile birds. Almost any larger-sized parrot, and even most smaller ones, tend to be more aggressive than cockatiels. You may find that it is better to avoid introductions with other animals in order to ensure that your cockatiel is safe. As with other predatory pets such as ferrets, snakes, and certain lizards, as well as dogs and cats, maintaining a "separate but equal" policy in your household may be helpful. Each animal will get some of your attention, just not at the same time.

Mutual interest in each other can be the beginning of a long-lasting friendship.

The Proper Diet

Pet stores sell ready-made seed mixtures for cockatiels that resemble what the birds would eat in the wild.

A seed mixture should consist of small seeds, such as various kinds of millet, canary seed, and canola seed. Larger seeds, such as hulled oats, wheat berries, buckwheat, hemp seed, and saf-flower seed are added. Sunflower seeds and nuts should be given only sparingly because they are high in fat and may lead to obesity. They also satisfy a bird's appetite too quickly. By contrast, small seeds are high in carbohy-drates and stimulate intestinal activity, and, because they are small, the cockatiel has to eat

Rowanberries add variety to the diet, and this female seems to find them tasty.

more of them, which keeps the bird occupied and entertained.

Freshness of the food is especially important. The older seeds or grain are, the less their nutritional value. A good way to check the freshness is to test for viability. Try sprouting a sample every so often (see page 32).

Spoiled food threatens the health of your cockatiel.

✔ Seeds high in fat, such as hemp and sunflower seeds, can get rancid.

✔ You can tell mildew by the whitish gray coating on the seeds and a sharp smell.

✔ Rotten food also smells bad and is slimy to the touch.

✔ Meal moths are harmless for the birds. You can tell they are present if the grains are clumped together as though with fine threads.

The basic rule is to store birdseed in an airy, dry place.

Spray millet is an easily digestible treat that young or sick birds enjoy particularly. It is also an important supplement to the diet for breeding pairs. A healthy cockatiel should get at most about 2 inches (5 cm) a day.

Seeds glued to heart or ring shapes with honey help keep a bird occupied, but they are loaded with calories. Fresh branches the bird can nibble on serve the same purpose much better.

Drinking water: You can simply use the water from your tap. Pet stores also sell "bird drink," or you can buy uncarbonated mineral water low in sodium. The water dish must be cleaned and refilled every day.

The Right Amount of Food

✔ The basic guideline is one to two tablespoons of seed per bird per day.

✔ Since birds have a high rate of metabolism and low stores of energy, it is important for them to eat small amounts frequently.

✔ To be on the safe side, always give a little more than the required daily ration.

✔ Remove empty husks by blowing them off before adding new seeds.

Important: Don't try to keep your bird at an optimal weight by limiting its food intake. In case of illness, the body's metabolism speeds up, and the bird needs more energy. If it can't get it by eating more, its state of health will rapidly decline. It is better to control weight by providing for more exercise.

Checklist
Feeding Rules

1 Feed the bird daily and, if possible, always at the same time.

2 Always give a little more food than necessary. However, there is no need for heaping dishes or more than one dish for the same food.

3 Fruits, vegetables, and greens should be given daily and must always be fresh. Put them in a separate dish. You may mix fruit in with wet food or sprouts.

4 Always wash and preferably peel fruit that is not from your own garden or from a farm you know; then let the water drip off.

5 Give only small amounts of leafy plants, such as lettuce, because they may contain pesticides in dissolved form.

6 Regularly offer fresh branches, nibble sticks, or a limestone block. The nibble sticks to which seeds are glued with honey are high in calories. Give them only rarely.

7 Offer food, especially treats, frequently from your hand. This encourages the cockatiel to become tame.

Scraps from the Table

Not suitable:
✔ Pretzels and chips because too much salt and fat are bad for liver and kidneys.
✔ Chocolate, candy, and cookies have too much fat, sugar, and artificial coloring.
✔ Alcohol and coffee.
Acceptable:
✔ Fruit juice containing no sugar.
✔ Dry bread, whole wheat crackers, whole grain breakfast cereals.
✔ Cooked potatoes and pasta, but not too hot.
✔ Lean meat.
✔ Occasionally yogurt, low-fat cottage cheese, or a very small amount of mild cheese.
✔ Black tea but only for a short time as an emergency measure against diarrhea.

Preparing Sprouts

Making sprouts takes a little extra time but has many advantages.
✔ Sprouts have more vitamins than other foods and are more easily digested.
✔ For raising young, parent birds need sprouted or soaked seeds.
✔ The swelling and sprouting process opens up the seeds and increases the vitamins and other nutrients contained in them.
✔ Rinsing under running water removes dust and dirt from the seeds.
✔ For young birds, sprouted seeds are easier to hull and eat.

To soak seeds, place them in a small bowl (you can use your commercial seed mixture, perhaps adding some corn, beans, peas, and oats) and cover them with water. After 12 hours rinse the seeds well. You can now mix in some fruit, add some egg food (available at pet stores), and give the food to your cockatiel.

To sprout seeds, you have to soak the swelled seeds again and rinse them again after 12 hours. Then you put them in a sieve placed in a dish and cover with a plate so they won't dry out. Let the seeds stand at room temperature another 24 to 48 hours, until they have started to sprout. If you want to give your bird sprouts every day, you will have to start several batches, one a day. Seeds that have gotten too dry don't sprout well, but they can be given just soaked.

Important: If any seeds begin to rot while sprouting, don't feed that batch to the bird.

Fruits and Vegetables

You can offer your bird just about any fruits and vegetables except cabbage, potatoes, avocados, and citrus fruit. In addition, you can give herbs and wild greens, such as basil, parsley, chervil, meadow grass, cow vetch, dandelion (leaves and stalks), sorrel, shepherd's purse, and watercress.

What is important is that the plants be unsprayed. If you buy fruits or vegetables, wash them thoroughly and, where appropriate, peel.

Keep in mind when feeding:
✔ Offer plenty of variety.
✔ If a bird refuses a particular food, keep offering it nevertheless.
✔ The chunks should not be too big; the cockatiel must be able to move them with its tongue.
✔ Pieces that are too small lose their texture quickly and get mushy.
✔ Offer fruits and vegetables in a separate dish or combined with soaked or sprouted

seeds, but the bird always has to have a separate dish with dry seeds available as well.

✔ Give citrus fruits only rarely, cabbage and raw potatoes not at all.

✔ Watch out with lettuce. Because of its high water content, lettuce may contain traces of many pesticides. If you grow your own lettuce organically you can give small amounts of it without worrying.

✔ Fasten greens to the cage bars with a clothespin (not the spring type).

Vitamins

Since there is no way of knowing how many vitamins your bird gets in its fresh food, you should add vitamins to its drinking water several times a week. Ask your veterinarian to recommend a good vitamin supplement for birds.

Follow the printed recommendations; giving too much of the supplement can be harmful. Since parrots in particular drink very little, the concentration of the vitamins in the water has to be relatively high.

Adding vitamins to soft food rather than water might be advisable because cockatiels do not drink that much water. Also, bacteria can grow quickly in water that has been enriched with vitamins.

Minerals and Trace Elements

These substances are necessary to maintain strong bones and a healthy plumage; young birds need them for growth, and females for

egg production. Some minerals are present in the food but others have to be added. When you buy mineral powder, make sure that it contains the substances necessary for skeletal growth and the formation of feathers; this information should appear on the product's label.

In nature, birds absorb minerals by eating some earth. As a substitute you should give your cockatiel bird grit. This is a mixture of different kinds of rock, seashells, oyster shells, cuttlefish, and limestone. You can also buy a mineral powder that you mix in the bird's food.

Food Pellets

These pellets contain all the nutrients a bird needs in the right amounts, but since eating them requires no work, the bird will soon grow lethargic and then will often refuse the pellets. A bird fed on pellets has all the more time to be bored.

The manufacturers of pellets themselves suggest providing entertainment and exercise for the bird after it eats. I recommend pellets only in the case of illness, when they are useful as a quick and easy source of energy. Pellets can be incorporated into the bird's daily food as a nutritious way to add variety to the diet.

Fruits and vegetables are an important source of vitamins for cockatiels.

HOW-TO: GROOMING

The Importance of Cleanliness

Your own hygienic precautions in dealings with the bird are just as important as the bird's needs for cleanliness. However, excessive fear of disease is unfounded because the droppings of a bird that is kept indoors are rarely contaminated with bacteria.

Following normal rules of cleanliness, such as keeping the cage clean and washing your hands regularly, is sufficient precaution. Keep in mind that exaggerated cleanliness, not to mention frequent disinfecting, weakens the bird's immune system. Many cleansers are toxic or irritate a bird's respiratory organs. If you are worried about disease, speak with your doctor or veterinarian.

Here are a few tips on cleaning up:
✔ Remove droppings on furniture immediately with a damp cloth.
✔ Let droppings on rugs dry, then pick them up with a paper towel.
✔ Droppings on clothing are best removed by brushing.

If your bird likes to perch on your shoulder, it may leave a stain now and then.

Warm water from a spray bottle is a substitute for rain.

The Bird Bath

Most cockatiels enjoy taking a bath in the form of a shower. They spread their wings so that the water can reach all parts of the body. Birds will often hang upside down from the roof of the cage or aviary in order to catch every drop of water from above. Baths enhance the birds' well-being, give them something to do, and stimulate the preening impulse. Give your cockatiel the chance to bathe as often as possible,

A cockatiel performs its own pedicure.

particularly in winter, when the birds suffer from the dry air of our heated houses.

Baths should be given during the day, preferably in the morning, to give the bird enough time to dry off and put its feathers back in order. Never get a bird wet and then turn off the light in the room. The bird would catch cold. You can imitate the natural summer rain by using a spray bottle or mister sold for watering plants. But be sure no trace of chemicals is in the bottle. Fill the bottle with hot water from the tap and set the valve on very fine.

The spray coming from the valve will be hand-warm. Now spray the bird from all sides. Do not spray the bird with anything other than water; chemicals can irritate the skin.

This is what the feathers of a well-groomed cockatiel look like.

The Bathhouse

If your bird likes to take a tub bath, perhaps in a relatively wide clay bowl that is not too deep or in a bathhouse for parrots sold at pet stores, it can decide for itself when to bathe. Some birds also like to take baths in a bowl with wet leaves. Just make sure the leaves come from unsprayed trees.

Not all cockatiels take to a bathhouse; some prefer showers.

Cleaning Schedule

Daily Chores	✔ Empty and clean food and water dishes. ✔ Replenish food and water. ✔ Remove big droppings with a spatula. ✔ Check bird for signs of illness. Observe its behavior, including how much it eats and drinks.
Weekly Chores	✔ Empty clean-out drawer; wash and dry it. ✔ Spread new grit on cage bottom and underneath climbing tree. ✔ Wash branches of climbing tree and perches in cage. ✔ Remove feathers and feather dust.
Monthly Chores	✔ Scrub cage bars and hose cage down with hot water. ✔ Remove top layer (about ¾ inch or 2 cm) of grit underneath climbing tree.

Information on Breeding

In the United States, each state varies in its regulations concerning the breeding of birds. Your state's local branch of the Department of Agriculture should know what is required by that state, and should have necessary information about any banding laws. Other organizations that might be able to supply information would include the American Federation of Aviculture (AFA) or the Humane Society.

The Breeding Cage

Cockatiels are relatively easy to breed and can be raised in almost any kind of cage, but it should be large enough to accommodate not only the nest box but for a while the young birds as well. The larger the cage, the better. An aviary would be ideal.

If you mount the nest box so it hangs outside the cage, the birds have some extra room and you will also find it easier to do the necessary nest checking.

Nest boxes are sold in two shapes, tall and squat. In the tall ones, the floor area should be 10 × 12 × 12 inches (26 × 30 × 30 cm), and the walls should be 13 to 15 inches (33 to 38 cm) high. The squat ones measure about 12 × 16 inches (30 × 40 cm) and are 10 inches (25 cm) high. The bottom board should have a thickness of 1³/₈ inches (3.5 cm); the side walls can be thinner.

For all types of nest boxes:

✔ The entry hole has to have a diameter of 3¹/₈ to 3¹/₂ inches (8 to 9 cm).

✔ Put a layer of wood shavings and some peat moss in the bottom of the box as nesting material.

✔ Since many females remove the litter, it is a good idea to carve a hollow in the floor of the box to keep the eggs from rolling away from under the brooding female.

✔ Nesting material and the nest box have to be made of untreated wood.

✔ Provide a climbing aid below the entry hole on the inside of the box. This can be a small wooden ladder or a few wooden blocks.

✔ The top has to be removable or hinged so you can check the inside of the box.

Very popular are nest boxes made of a hollowed-out piece of tree trunk. They offer a better microclimate, and the natural rough surface of the interior makes it easier for the birds to climb up and down. Here, too, be sure the wood is untreated.

The Breeding Pair

For a successful mating you have to have a sexually mature and congenial pair of birds. For information on sexing cockatiels, see page 12. Although cockatiels reach sexual maturity at seven to nine months, you should wait until they are about a year old before breeding them the first time.

A pair generally stays together for life. They are quite tolerant toward other pairs and single birds. Fights arise only if a bird that already has a mate is wooed by another bird or if two pairs want to use the same nest box. To avoid these problems, keep an equal number of males and females in a communal aviary, and provide more nest boxes than pairs of birds.

Observation during Courtship

When two birds have taken a liking to each other, they sit close to each other. They can now be considered engaged, and from now on they will do almost everything together. The male also scratches the female's head and gives her kisses.

To solidify the pair bond, the male performs a courtship song in the form of a melodic and rhythmical whistling. Now and then he runs back and forth on a perch with spread wings, banging on it every so often with his beak to impress the female. Quite often he raises his crest as he does this. Then he walks around the female with mincing steps, showing off his white wing patches, bowing to her repeatedly, and spreading his tail feathers into a fan.

Egg Laying and Brooding

The female starts laying eggs about a week after the mating has taken place. Every two days she lays an egg, eventually producing four to six eggs, occasionally more. Although both parents spend a lot of time in the box, they often don't start sitting until after the third egg. The female usually broods the eggs at night and, if necessary, during the day as well, depending on the willingness of the male to sit on the eggs.

Extensive mutual preening strengthens the pair bond.

About 18 to 21 days after the first egg appears, the chicks hatch, in the same order as the eggs were laid. The younger birds in the clutch are smaller than their siblings but generally receive the same care from the parents as the bigger ones.

Tips for Incubation

✔ The birds need quiet now. Do as little as possible in or near the nest box in order not to bother the parents. Young pairs often leave the nest if they are disturbed.

✔ If possible, wait with nest checks until no parent bird is in the box. The birds are quite protective of their brood.

✔ An even temperature of about 72°F (22°C) and a humidity of about 60 percent will contribute to good hatching results.

✔ You can check to see if the eggs are fertile by candling them with a strong light bulb. Fertile eggs show a network of blood vessels after about eight days; later they become opaque. Infertile eggs are clear, but rotting eggs are dark, too.

✔ Don't remove infertile eggs right away, or the female may start laying more; also, these eggs often serve as support to the chicks and help keep them warm.

✔ Don't clean off dirty eggs; they are covered with a protective film.

✔ If the clutch is large and the nest box gets very dirty after a while, set the nestlings in a bowl and replace the litter in the box. But don't do this too often.

✔ Give the parent birds rearing food while they are brooding. This is a nutritious sprouted food with added animal proteins, such as hard-boiled egg, commercial egg food, or soft food for insectivorous birds.

✔ Do not give the birds food that they have never seen before. If you plan to breed the birds, get them used to rearing food before the eggs are laid. As soon as the first egg is laid, be sure to add calcium to the food. Female cockatiels easily become calcium depleted. Simply supplying a cuttlebone often is not enough because the female may be chewing it up without actually eating any of it. A calcium-depleted female is prone to egg binding.

Unplanned Brooding

Even a female kept singly can produce eggs. If this happens, do not remove the eggs

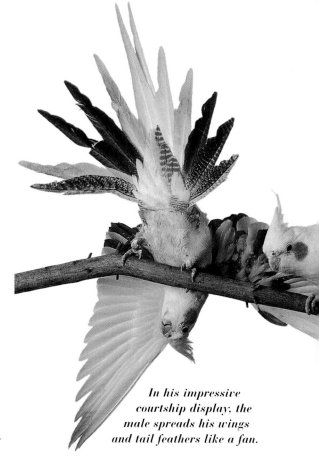

In his impressive courtship display, the male spreads his wings and tail feathers like a fan.

because the female will immediately lay more eggs to replace the ones that are gone. This puts a greater strain on the bird's system than sitting on the eggs.

If you have a pair that you don't want to breed, don't supply a nest box. If the female lays eggs all the same, leave them for the sake of the female bird, but punch a hole in both ends of the eggs with a thick needle. This will keep embryos from forming. You can also replace the eggs with artificial ones. When the female leaves the nest after a while, you can remove the eggs.

The Development of Baby Birds

Age	Weight	Appearance	Behavior
Newly hatched	About 4-5 grams	Pink skin covered with yellow down; eyes closed; feet, beak, and claws flesh-colored; lower mandible broad like a small shovel	Cannot sit or raise head; are fed an almost liquid substance, the so-called crop milk
4th to 5th day	About 15 grams	Eyes begin to open	Clearly audible begging calls
10th day	About 35 grams	Eyes fully open; the first small feathers appear; first crest feathers visible on head	Can raise head and hiss softly; are being fed more and more predigested seeds; make pumping motions when begging for food
12th to 27th day	40-60 grams	Lose the egg tooth; beak has hardened; first quills break open and sometimes reveal later feather color	Recognize parents; hiss at strangers they take for enemies
28th to 35th day	About 80 grams	Feathers almost completely formed; colors somewhat fainter than in adult birds	Flap their wings in the nest box; leave the box soon after even though they cannot fly right away, having to practice first
About 35 to 40 days	80–100 grams	Plumage is complete	Begin to eat on their own; parents feed them less and less
About 6 months	80–100 grams	Molt replaces juvenile with brighter adult plumage	Completely independent
9 months	80–100 grams	Adult coloration	Sexually mature

BEHAVIOR AND ACTIVITIES

Cockatiels have been living in captivity for a long time and are considered domesticated. They have retained a number of behavior patterns from their natural state that you should know about to help you understand your bird and keep it well occupied.

The Curious Cockatiel

There is hardly a creature as curious about everything around it as a tame cockatiel. Anything that looks at all interesting, makes the slightest noise, or is attractive for some other reason is checked out and investigated thoroughly. This makes sense in the cockatiel's Australian homeland, where the birds have to pay attention to the changing conditions of their environment and adjust to them. In your home, this natural behavior can give rise to comical situations but also put the bird in real danger.

✔ If you flush the toilet in the bird's presence, it will watch intently, trying to figure out where the water comes from. Should it bend too far over the rim of the bowl it could slip in and possibly drown—if you are not there watching.

✔ After a thorough visual inspection, the bird will explore any new object with the beak and the tongue. This can have disastrous effects if the object is a hot iron or contains poisonous substances.

Once a pair bond has formed, the two birds will do everything together.

✔ If certain things happen repeatedly in a certain way, the cockatiel will quickly grasp the principle involved. Thus, a bird will not take long to figure out how and through what opening it leaves the cage. If the cage door is locked it will patiently investigate the lock, and if the lock isn't too tricky the bird may figure out how to undo it and decide to take a spin in the room on its own. If the window happens to be open, there is, of course, a special danger of escape.

Typical Activities

Preening is one of the most important activities for birds in the wild, for only a plumage in prime condition protects against inclement weather and allows quick escape from predators. Birds in captivity, too, preen themselves several times a day. A cockatiel can easily spend two to three hours, but with interruptions, cleaning, sorting, and rearranging its feathers. Each feather is drawn through the beak to free it of dust and dirt and smooth it. Then oil and powder are applied to make the plumage waterproof. That is why birds can fly in the rain without getting soaked and cold. The oil is produced in a special gland just above the base of the tail, called the uropygial or oil gland. The bird picks up the oily secretion with its beak and distributes it evenly over the plumage. The head, which is out of the beak's reach, is rubbed directly over the gland. The powder comes from "powder down."

Scratching is another normal daily activity. It serves the purpose of removing particles of dirt and relieving itches. If your bird keeps scratching the same spot a lot, you should consult the veterinarian to find out the reason. Perhaps your bird has parasites (see page 53). Cockatiels scratch their heads by raising the foot under the wing.

Shaking the feathers is something you will see your cockatiel do several times a day, especially in the morning. A shaking motion runs along the whole body, often producing a rustling sound. Shaking serves, first of all, to get rid of dust and, secondly, to get all the feathers to lie where they belong, so that the plumage is in top condition for quick takeoff, if necessary. Birds will also shake themselves to relieve tension after an exciting or upsetting experience.

A brief fluffing of the mask, that is, a raising of the head feathers, may be a reaction to an unfamiliar event, or if the bird is mildly irritated, such as by a noise or an annoying light. Cockatiels are able to fluff up or raise just these feathers. Young birds, especially, look cute when they do this because it makes the head look even rounder than usual. Adult birds as well as juveniles raise the head feathers shortly before going to sleep or while dozing.

When the bird fluffs its entire plumage, all the feathers of the body stand up. They no longer hug the body and, instead, create a kind of insulating air cushion. Cockatiels fluff themselves up primarily when they are cold, but sometimes also for sleeping. If a bird sits in one

Cockatiels display true acrobatics to get at food they like.

place all day with puffed-up feathers when it is not particularly cold, this is a sign of possible illness that should not be ignored. Such a bird will often rest on both legs instead of on just one, out of weakness.

Beak whetting is always done after a meal but sometimes at other times of day as well. The bird rubs its beak against a cage bar or, preferably, against a branch or twig. Natural branches are best for this. Beak whetting serves to remove bits of leftover food, especially fruit and egg food, that tends to stick to the beak. The bird may also whet its beak in situations it perceives as difficult or threatening. This apparently irrelevant reaction, called a displacement activity, may

Eating is one way for a cockatiel to keep busy.

diffuse anxiety associated with a particular situation. The physical purpose is to smooth out minor irregularities in the beak surface.

Whetting the beak can also be a form of greeting, as, for example, when you return after a prolonged absence. By making similar motions against a branch with your fingernail, you can approximate the response another cockatiel would make to this gesture.

Yawning is something all parrots do. They generally yawn when a lack of oxygen makes them feel sleepy. Birds that are kept indoors are very sensitive to stale air. If you see your cockatiel yawning during the day, air the room thoroughly.

Yawning can also be a way for a bird to adjust the contents of its crop. It is not unusual for a cockatiel to awaken from its post-meal nap and yawn several times. This helps to mix

the food with the bird's digestive enzymes, which then helps the food move down the digestive tract.

When sneezing, cockatiels sound very much like a person sneezing. A cockatiel's sneezing is more like our nose blowing, a way to clear the nasal passages. This type of sneezing often occurs during preening when the bird gets powder or bits of feather in its nose.

Sneezing can also indicate a sinus infection. While cockatiels rarely get a "runny nose," a sinus infection is usually accompanied by reddened, enlarged nostrils. The bird also may seem "off" or not quite its usual perky self.

UNDERSTANDING
BEHAVIOR

In order to understand your cockatiel's language you have to be able to interpret its behavior accurately.

 This is what my cockatiel does.

 What is it expressing by doing this?

 How do I respond to its behavior?

☝ The bird is pulling a feather through its beak.

❓ It is cleaning and smoothing the feather.

❗ If no feathers are pulled out, leave the bird alone.

☝ These two cockatiels are screaming at each other.

❓ They are engaged in a quarrel.

❗ If the quarrel turns into a serious fight, you have to intervene and separate the birds.

☝ This cockatiel is scratching its head.

❓ It is preening itself.

❗ If the bird is not scratching only one spot, this is part of the daily routine.

☝ This bird is stretching one wing and one leg.

❓ It has finished one activity, such as preening.

❗ Devote some time to your bird now; it is feeling relaxed.

These birds are sitting close to each other, with their plumage slightly raised.

They want to take a nap together.

Please, don't disturb for a while.

One bird is scratching the other's neck.

This is how cockatiels express their affection for each other.

Watch the pair. If it seems indicated, make a nest box available.

Two birds are preening at the same time.

This social behavior suggests that they are a mated pair.

Enjoy watching their interactions without disturbing the birds.

This bird is shaking itself with a rustling noise.

It is getting the feathers to lie in their proper place.

Now it is ready for action. Play with it.

This cockatiel is raising its wings.

It is stretching its muscles.

Offer it an opportunity to fly.

Movements and Postures

You will often observe the following movements in your cockatiel:

Stretching the legs is a typical movement, in which one leg together with the wing of the same side is stretched backward and then returned to normal position. The toes are curled up during the stretch. This movement is comparable to our stretching. It relaxes tired leg muscles and other parts of the body.

Tucking the beak in the back feathers is another typical gesture. Cockatiels sleep in this position if they feel safe. The head is rotated 180 degrees, and the beak is buried in the slightly fluffed-up back feathers.

Birds also swivel their heads a full 180 degrees when they preen the feathers of the back.

Resting on one leg serves to take the weight off the other leg and relax it. Birds often sleep standing on one leg, and they often rest during the day by pulling one leg up. Birds kept in an outdoor aviary also pull up one leg at a time to keep warm when the weather gets cold. Cockatiels missing one leg should therefore not be kept outdoors in the winter.

Cockatiels look especially comical when they stretch a leg backward and then bring it forward with a theatrical flourish to tuck it into the abdominal feathers.

Raising both wings simultaneously is another exercise that serves as relaxation. Your bird will also raise its wings when it is very hot in order to release body heat. The same behavior is displayed in a very different situation, namely, during a luxurious shower when the bird tries to expose as much of its body as possible to the water.

Spreading both wings sideways is part of the male's courtship display behavior (see page 36). It is meant to impress the chosen female and arouse her admiration. The head is lowered, the body kept erect at a steep angle, and the tail pointed upward. If your cockatiel has become imprinted to humans, it may woo you by assuming this posture. Take it as a compliment.

The completely erect crest is a sign of the male's excitement as it woos the female.

Sensory Perceptions

Vision is the most highly developed sense of cockatiels. In captivity, as in nature, cockatiels feel most secure when they can survey their surroundings from an

What the Crest Tells You

Position of the Crest	What Does It Mean?
The crest lies almost flat on the head with the tip pointing slightly upward. The plumage is completely smooth.	The bird is calm and relaxed.
The crest is raised vertically.	The bird is busy with something that absorbs its attention. It is interested, perhaps investigating some new object.
The crest is raised as far as it will go, almost pointing forward.	This is a sign of great excitement and tension, as well as of concentration.
The cockatiel snaps its crest back and hisses; the head is stretched forward.	The bird is anxious and insecure; it is afraid of something.

elevated perch so that they can detect a potential enemy in good time to hide or flee. That is why a cage should never be placed low.

Cockatiels initially respond to anything new in their surroundings with skepticism, but after a while this often gives way to curiosity. Any new object is watched closely before it is accepted so it is better not to make changes in the bird's surroundings during the acclimation phase. The same applies to the clothing you wear.

The perception of color is quite highly developed in birds because color plays such an important role in their natural environment: in the wooing of a mate, the search for food, and the recognition of predators. As in many animals, the eyes are placed on the side of the head for panoramic vision; consequently, cockatiels can see what is happening behind their backs.

In order not to miss anything in their rapid flight, birds have the ability to register and process about five times as many images per second as humans.

The sense of hearing is also well developed. Cockatiels need to hear well to be able to communicate with each other in nature across long distances. The range of sounds they hear is almost the same as for humans. Sounds a cockatiel hears often and that are therefore familiar don't arouse its attention, but unfamiliar ones can scare a bird even if they are not at all loud. Classical music seems to be soothing if played softly. The vacuum cleaner, on the other hand, may elicit cries of displeasure.

The sense of taste is not very important for birds living in the wild. Birds learn what is suitable for eating from their parents. Individual experience can also play a role. The selection of available food is, of course, not great enough in the cockatiels' homeland for the birds to be very selective. Wild cockatiels usually check food out with their tongue and spit out what is inedible before they really taste it.

The position of the crest indicates that this bird is examining the contents of the basket with great concentration.

Birds in captivity can be quite finicky about what they eat and may test your patience with their determination to eat only what they like. Apparently almost all cage birds like salt. You can therefore include a piece of pretzel now and then in the menu. But caution is in order: Too much salt is bad for the kidneys. In the wild, birds satisfy their need for salt by eating earth and plants containing minerals.

We know very little about the sense of smell in birds, but it seems likely that birds perceive some smells, such as that of smoke and of substances with a strong, irritating odor. For this reason, if for no other, you should not smoke in the vicinity of birds.

Vocalizations

If a cockatiel feels threatened, if something bothers it, or if, in the case of a male, it is performing a courtship display, it can become quite vociferous. This has earned cockatiels the reputation among aviculturists of being very noisy. In fact, cockatiels are unpleasantly loud only in certain situations or if kept singly. Most of the time cockatiels communicate with each other and with humans in relatively quiet tones.

Cockatiels answer the calls of their fellows and respond to the words of their caretakers. The contact calls uttered in flight are quite audible and serve the cohesion of the flock. The hissing sound produced not only by adults but by young birds as well is meant to ward off enemies. But it is not particularly loud.

Screamers are usually birds that have suffered severe neglect and feel lonely and bored. If your bird is a screamer you should review its living conditions, and if you can't improve them you might do well to pass the bird on to someone who can offer it a more suitable environment. Another possibility is to get a second bird as a companion.

If the bird feels happy in your home you will never consider its vocal communications with you unpleasant. A cockatiel always greets its keeper with a cry of pleasure, and when you leave the room it will give voice to disappointment.

You can try to encourage your cockatiel's vocal mimicking by saying a word or phrase repeatedly whenever a certain situation arises. For example, say Good morning every day when you enter the room where the bird is kept. Or perhaps your cockatiel has a talent for whistling. You might want to try whistling the same basic tune over and over to see if your bird can mimic you. Whenever you try to teach your cockatiel something new, make sure there are limited distractions around you.

This bird is scrutinizing its mirror image, which it takes to be a fellow cockatiel.

TIP

Fun Observations

A new toy will be eyed suspiciously when it is first introduced. Watch the position of the cockatiel's crest as the bird gets acquainted with the new object. Quite often the first response will be hissing. But once the bird realizes that the toy is harmless it will investigate it, nibbling on it and feeling it with the tongue. While thus occupied, it almost forgets the world around it and will occasionally emit soft squeaking sounds.

The cockatiel will react similarly to changes in the room where it is allowed to fly. Such changes introduce variety into the daily routine, but don't overdo it. The bird can become stressed if it must constantly adjust to innovations.

Play

To keep a cockatiel's mental capabilities from deteriorating, it is advisable to keep at least two birds. If that is impossible, make it a point to interact a lot with your one bird. If you don't have the time, supply toys to introduce some variety into the bird's life.

Wooden toys such as rings, ladders, or spools strung on a small chain are very popular.

Mirrors give the bird the impression that there is another bird present. Mirrors made of glass break easily, so you should choose a metal one. A metal mirror can also be used by the bird to make noise.

Small bells also make charming toys for cockatiels.

Cardboard boxes and snippets of paper as well as cardboard toilet paper tubes provide entertainment at no cost. A cockatiel may spend hours reducing paper to confetti but don't give it printed paper because of the ink.

A ladder made of wooden rungs and sisal twine is a favorite plaything that can be utilized in all kinds of ways.

Togetherness Is Everything

When you are at home you should include your tame cockatiel in your activities.

✔ Give the bird something to occupy it while you do your housekeeping chores.

✔ When it's time to set the table, some birds like to move the silverware around for the

Cockatiels are full of curiosity.

noise it makes. On the other hand, many birds are afraid of the noisy vacuum cleaner. If this is the case with your bird, talk to it reassuringly and place it in its cage. Soon it will realize that the vacuum cleaner is harmless and may retreat to the cage on its own at the sight of the thing.

If the bird does something you don't like, say *"No"* emphatically. Quite often this will stop the bird. If you are

Tame cockatiels like as much physical contact with their keepers as possible.

consistent, your *"No"* eventually may be enough to keep the bird from doing things you don't approve of.

Cockatiels like to pass the time climbing and doing acrobatics.

Thick strings animate the bird to do gymnastics and to use them as swings.

Wooden pencils get bitten to pieces. Use twigs from fruit trees to distract the bird from pencils.

Climbing trees (available at pet stores) are a great success with birds. If you hang toys from the branches, the tree becomes even more interesting. The tree should have a permanent location at some distance from the cage so that the bird has to fly to it. But leave the bird in the tree only while you are in the same room.

Learning to Talk

Whistling notes or entire tunes they hear is something many cockatiels excel at. You can develop this talent in your bird by whistling the same melody for it over and over.

The ability to talk is not so impressive in cockatiels, but there are ways to bring to light a hidden talent if it exists and to further it.

✔ Repeat the words you would like the bird to say as often as possible.

✔ Always use the same tone of voice and the same words for a particular situation.

✔ Proceed one step at a time. Let the bird learn one word or phrase; once it knows that, go on to the next word.

✔ Try to eliminate distractions during the lessons.

✔ The bird will concentrate best while it sits on your hand.

✔ If there are times when the bird doesn't cooperate, don't lose patience and give up.

✔ Don't force your cockatiel to mimic speech. If it has no gift at all in this area, enjoy its company in other ways.

Children enjoy playing with a tame bird, and the pleasure is mutual.

PREVENTIVE HEALTH CARE AND ILLNESS

Even if you offer optimal conditions, take excellent care of your bird, and provide a healthy diet, your cockatiel may, like any other creature, eventually get sick. This chapter tells you how to prevent and treat diseases and how to care for a sick bird.

An Ounce of Prevention

Prevention is especially important in the case of birds because they give very little sign of being sick. By the time you notice that something is wrong, it may already by too late.

How well fed a bird is plays a large role in overcoming illness. Cockatiels put on hardly any fat, and a sick or weakened bird often stops eating. This is doubly dangerous because most illnesses are accompanied by weight loss.

Injuries

Injuries result from encounters with cats or other animals or from fights over nest sites or rank, as well as from carelessness when the bird flies free (see page 23).

Symptoms of injury: Blood on the plumage and/or perch. Even if there is very little blood, you should examine the bird thoroughly.

Minor wounds heal by themselves. If the bleeding is heavy, try to stop it by applying

Only a bird that is healthy stretches and relaxes like this.

gentle pressure and take the bird to the veterinarian as quickly as possible.

Iodine solutions (water-based) can be used to clean minor cuts. Styptic powder should be used only on toenails that have been trimmed too closely.

Parasites

The most likely parasites are red bird mites, feather mites, lice, and burrowing mites. These are usually picked up through contact with other birds.

Red bird mites manifest themselves in a bird's restlessness, especially at night (that is when they suck blood), and compulsive preening. Get medication from the veterinarian and thoroughly clean all wooden objects in the cage or get rid of them altogether. Do the same if the bird has feather mites.

Burrowing mites cause so-called parrot mange. The mites live on all parts of the bird not covered by feathers. There they burrow into the skin, causing welts.

Parasites are very uncommon in the United States, but an avian veterinarian should immediately check any suspicion of an infestation.

Skin and Plumage Diseases

If the claws and beak are growing too long, don't simply trim them because this stimulates further growth. Hang a whetting stone in the cage for the beak and offer fresh branches frequently for chewing. Claws get worn down best on branches of varying thickness. If you do have to reach for the clippers, proceed with caution; cutting too far back causes bleeding. For information on stopping bleeding, see page 53.

Malformation of feathers may be genetic or the result of inadequate diet or a metabolic disorder. There is not much you can do about it. If the abnormal feather isn't bothering the bird, leave it alone. If it interferes with the bird's well-being, consult the veterinarian.

Skin changes, such as thickening or growths, can have many causes.

✔ Fatty lumps are harmless and are quite frequent in older birds. In the early stages they can sometimes be surgically removed.

✔ Cysts in the feather follicles are feathers that keep growing in or under the skin. They have to be taken care of by the veterinarian.

✔ The oil gland above the base of the tail can sometimes get clogged and then gets infected.

Intestinal Tract Diseases

The droppings of birds are made up of feces (greenish brown), uric acid (white), and urine (clear liquid). If the white part is watery, it is a sign of kidney problems.

In the case of diarrhea, the greenish brown part of the dropping is runny, and the feathers near the cloaca are soiled. The droppings may be bloody, and the bird may sit around apathetically. If diarrhea persists for a whole day the bird loses a lot of fluid and hardly absorbs any energy from its food. There are a number of possible causes, including spoiled food, ingestion of poisonous substances (see pages 25, 27),

and bacteria. In order for the disease not to spread you should separate the afflicted bird and keep it under a red heat lamp until you can get it to the veterinarian. Temporarily eliminate fruit and fresh food from the diet and give the bird activated charcoal and chamomile tea. Glucose in the drinking water helps supply energy. Yogurt or, better yet, intestinal bacteria prescribed by the veterinarian can often eliminate the disease agents.

Attention: Large amounts of fruit in the diet can temporarily result in runny droppings because of the acid in the fruit.

Causes of constipation include inappropriate diet, ingestion of foreign objects, a tumor or swelling that closes off the cloaca, egg binding, and lack of exercise. Have the veterinarian determine the cause and prescribe treatment.

Crop inflammation prevents proper digestion of food. The first symptoms are

This female is proudly displaying her long primaries.

Recognizing Signs of Illness

What You Notice	Possible Causes You Can Remedy Yourself	Additional Symptoms Requiring a Prompt Trip to the Veterinarian
Refusal to eat	Spoiled food, satiety, wrong room temperature, aversion to certain foods	Diarrhea, vomiting, permanently puffed-up plumage
Choking up of seeds	Courtship display behavior, crop inflammation, parasite infestation	Breast feathers stuck together, weight loss, sour smell
Trouble breathing, noisy breathing	Exhaustion after exertion, hot weather, high room temperature, high humidity, obesity	Rattling sound in throat, squeaking or whistling noise (pneumonia, psittacosis, see page 57), fungus infection, tail whipping, hanging with beak from cage bars to get air, nasal discharge
Frequent sneezing	Dry, dusty air, penetrating smells, picking at nose with foot	Bad cold, psittacosis (see page 57), heavy discharge from nose (blood, pus), teary eyes
Loose droppings	Nervousness, too much fruit in diet, cold food or water, stress	Frothy bubbles, blood, abnormal color, puffed-up plumage, parasites, inflammation of intestinal tract
Unsuccessful efforts to defecate	Minor constipation	No droppings for prolonged period, cries of pain, intestinal blockage, tumor, serious constipation, egg binding
Constant scratching, restlessness	Dry air, lack of bathing water	Sleeplessness, apathy, feather pulling, self-mutilation, parasites, skin infection, skin fungus
Limping, favoring one leg and/or wing	Bruising, pulled muscle or ligament	Leg or wing hanging down limply, open wounds, broken bone, injured nerve

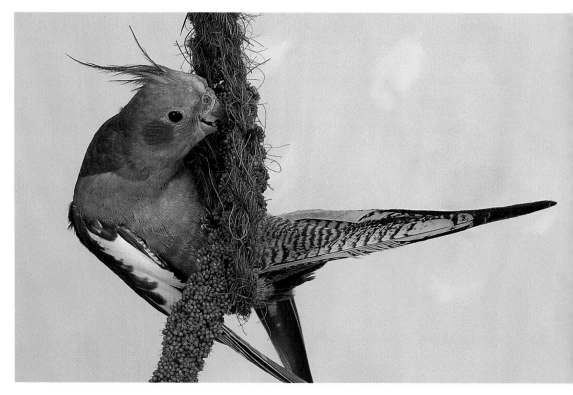

sneezing, vomiting of sour-smelling crop contents, and violent head shaking. Possible causes include swallowing of a foreign body, spoiled food, bacteria, and parasites. Take your bird to the veterinarian.

A cockatiel uses not only its feet but also its beak to hold on.

Illness from Trauma

A concussion is the consequence of flying against a window or of some other collision. Symptoms range from tilting the head to loss of consciousness. The first step is to place the injured bird in a quiet, darkened room. Avoid all commotion and shaking. Once the bird's state has stabilized, take it to the veterinarian.

Partial paralysis may be caused by vitamin deficiencies, a tumor, egg binding in which the egg presses on a nerve, calcium deficiency, a pulled ligament, or an ingrown ring. The ring can be removed with pliers. Egg binding or a tumor requires the attention of a veterinarian. A varied diet prevents nutritional deficiencies.

Fractures are often caused by accidents. A toe broken in a closing door usually mends by itself. A broken leg or wing, however, has to be set and splinted right away by the veterinarian to prevent the bones from fusing in the wrong position. The recuperating bird has to be kept absolutely quiet and may not move.

Respiratory Diseases

These can range from difficulty breathing, noisy breathing, and shortness of breath to pneumonia. Dry indoor air dries out the mucous membranes of the respiratory tract and makes it vulnerable to disease. Problems can also be triggered by drafts and cigarette smoke, as well as by bacteria and fungi. You can prevent the air from getting too dry by having a humidifier, a fountain, or an aquarium in the room.

Psittacosis is a serious health threat for people as well as birds. It is a bacterial infection manifested by a head cold, nasal discharge, conjunctivitis, and apathetic behavior. An affected cockatiel will sit with its plumage permanently puffed up. People suffering from the disease develop a high fever. Immediate medical attention is crucial.

Consulting the Veterinarian

If you notice a change in the appearance or behavior of your bird, consult a veterinarian.

Find out before an emergency arises where there is a second veterinarian (in case your regular one is unavailable) or if there is an emergency clinic.

✔ Transport your bird in its cage if the cage is not too large.

✔ If the cage is too large, put the bird in a transport box; a cockatiel can't hurt itself in such a box.

✔ Don't clean the cage before your visit to the veterinarian. He or she may want to analyze the droppings and check on the setup of the cage.

Checklist
Questions

1 About the bird's acquisition: How old is the bird? How long have you owned it? Where did you get it?

2 About the illness: What are the droppings like? (You may want to take a sample.) When did you first notice a change? What struck you in particular? Has the cockatiel had similar or other symptoms or diseases in the past? Has it been treated before and, if so, for how long and with what medication?

3 About the diet: What do you feed the bird? What does it drink? When did it last eat fresh food and what kind? Has there been a recent change in its diet?

4 About its environment: Does the bird have any contact with hazardous materials, such as paint, lead weights in the drapes, and so on? Do you have other birds or pets? Where is the cage located? Have any people the bird is in contact with gotten sick?

A sick bird will often sleep crouching on the ground.

You can tell that a bird is sick if it sits apathetically in a corner or on a perch with dull, glassy eyes.

Quarantine

If you keep several cockatiels and one of them comes down with a contagious disease, the sick bird should be segregated. Put it in a separate cage or a so-called "sick box," a cage that can be heated. If you have just one bird you can leave it in its regular cage.

The cage with the sick bird should be in a quiet, dry room with a temperature of 72–76°F (22 to 24°C). Avoid anything that might cause excitement or stress.

Giving Medication

Be sure to follow the vet-erinarian's directions concerning dosage. This is especially important if the medication has to be continued over some time. If you stop giving it too soon, the bird may suffer a relapse.

Medication in liquid or powder form is given in the drinking water. The concentration in the water has to be fairly high because parrots don't drink much, yet your bird has to swallow enough of the administered drug.

Powder can also be sprinkled over the birdseed but then you have to make sure the cockatiel can get only at the treated food. If you have a bird seriously weakened by illness, put the food and water very close by and spread some cloth on the cage bottom so that the bird doesn't hurt itself if it loses its balance.

Applying Ointments

Immobilize the bird with a towel and have another person dab the ointment on the required spot with a cotton swab. The fear that the cockatiel will resent and remember being caught and held steady is generally unfounded. Birds usually associate the unpleasant experience with the towel.

Giving eyedrops is done similarly, that is, by holding the bird with a towel and then dripping the medication into the eye.

Giving Medication Directly in the Beak

With a very weakened bird that doesn't eat or drink on its own, medication has to be given directly into the beak. Hold the bird loosely in a towel, then introduce the medication slowly into the beak with a disposable syringe. Give the bird time to swallow between doses.

If you have to force-feed, give the bird baby food in the same way. Here, too, you have to watch out that the bird is swallowing.

The best way to give a bird medicine is with a syringe.

Using a Heat Lamp

A heat lamp speeds recovery and is a source of warmth.

✔ Mount the lamp in such a way that the rays feel comfortable on your hand held at the same distance from the lamp as the bird will be.

✔ Water always has to be available.

✔ Keep the lamp on constantly.

✔ At night, darken the cage half that is not exposed to the rays with a cloth.

✔ When your cockatiel begins to feel better, turn the lamp off periodically at shorter and shorter intervals. The temperature in the room should drop only slowly.

Expose only half the cage to the heat lamp so that the bird can move to a cooler spot.

Disinfecting

In case of a contagious disease or after the successful conclusion of treatment, all the objects the patient had any contact with should be disinfected. Ask your veterinarian to recommend an appropriate product.

Helping Your Bird Regain Strength

Once an illness has been overcome, you should do everything you can to nurse your bird back to its former physical condition. Healthy and varied food, plenty of fresh air, and devoting special attention to the recuperating patient will achieve a great deal. Giving extra vitamins will enhance natural resistance.

Following Surgery

✔ Place the bird in a well-padded, darkened box until it wakes up.

✔ Avoid holding it in your hand because this often impedes breathing and tends to create anxiety.

✔ Make sure the bird lies in the box with the head stretched out straight. The bird should not be on its back.

✔ At home, place the bird in the sick box or cage and watch it for some time.

✔ After major surgery, make sure the bird is warm and undisturbed.

Emergency Kit

✔ Telephone number of the veterinarian

✔ Styptic cotton

✔ An iodine salve

✔ Glucose

✔ Small scissors, pliers, tweezers, magnifying glass

✔ Stretch bandage

Ointment is applied with a cotton swab.

Keep an eye on your bird while it is flying free; it might pick up a disease from something it swallows.

Organization

National Cockatiel Society (NCS)
11655 Emerald Drive
Hayden Lake, ID 83835
(208) 762-9123
www.cockatiels.org

The NCS is a nonprofit organization that provides information on proper care, handling, maintenance, and breeding; they have published articles on communication and social behavior.

Books for Further Reading

Barrie, Annmarie. *Beginners Guide to Cockatiels.* Neptune, NJ: TFH Publications, 1990.

Harris, Jack. *Cockatiels As a Hobby.* Neptune, NJ: TFH Publications, 1992.

Kelsey-Wood, Dennis. *Cockatiels Today.* Neptune, NJ: TFH Publications, 1996.

Tartak, Laura. *Cockatiels.* Neptune, NJ: TFH Publications, 1997.

Vriends, Matthew. *The New Cockatiel Handbook.* Hauppauge, NY: Barron's Educational Series, Inc., 1989.

Photos

Front cover: A Pearl, a Pied, and a Wild-type cockatiel.
Back cover: Wild-type cockatiel.
Page 1: Two Wild-type cockatiels.
Pages 2–3: A male Pied preening a female Pearl.
Pages 4–5: There is no jealousy over food between these two birds.
Pages 6–7: A Wild-type cockatiel contemplating lettuce leaves.
Page 64: Wild-type at left, Pearl at right.

Acknowledgments

The author wishes to express gratitude to his parents, who always actively supported his interests, and to his family, who enabled him to find the time to work on this book.

The photographer wants to thank Karl Gerbl and Sepp Christ for lending her their birds so she could take pictures of them; also Regina Wolf, Monika Dressel, and Birgit Kuhl and son Lukas for allowing her to photograph their cockatiels.

About the Author

Thomas Haupt grew up with animals and has been a practicing veterinarian since 1992. A fairly large proportion of his patients are birds. He keeps a number of birds himself, especially parrots of various species. Dr. Haupt also maintains an infirmary for injured wild animals.

About the Photographer

Karin Skogstad has been working as a freelance journalist and photographer since 1979, specializing in animals and plants.

The Artist

György Jankovics is a trained graphic artist and has studied at the art academies of Budapest and Hamburg. He does animal and plant illustrations for a number of major publishing houses.

Important Note

People allergic to feathers or feather dust should not keep birds. Consult your doctor before getting one.

Psittacosis is a bacterial infection that people can contract if they come in contact with the nasal secretion or inhale dust particles from the droppings of infected birds (see page 57). If you think your cockatiel might have psittacosis, have the veterinarian check it out, and if you have cold or flu symptoms, see your doctor and tell him or her that you keep birds.

English translation © Copyright 1999 by Barron's Educational Series, Inc.

Original title of the book in German is *Nymphensittiche*.

Copyright © 1998 by Gräfe und Unzer Verlag GmbH, Munich.

All inquiries should be addressed to:
Barron's Educational Series, Inc.
250 Wireless Boulevard
Hauppauge, New York 11788

http://www.barronseduc.com

Library of Congress Catalog Card No. 98-48070

International Standard Book No. 0-7641-0938-3

Library of Congress Cataloging-in-Publication Data
Haupt, Thomas.
    [Nymphensittiche.   English]
    Cockatiels : everything about purchase, care, nutrition, breeding and behavior / Thomas Haupt ; photographs, Karin Skogstad ; drawings, György Jankovics ; translated from the German by Rita Kimber.
        p.   cm. — (A complete pet owner's manual)
    Includes bibliographical references and index.
    ISBN 0-7641-0938-3
    1. Cockatiel. I. Title. II. Series.
SF473.C6H38513   1999
636.6'8656—dc21   98-48070
                                                          CIP

Printed in Hong Kong

9 8 7 6 5 4 3 2 1

EXPERT ADVICE

An expert answers the ten most frequently asked questions about keeping cockatiels as pets.

1 Should I keep just one or at least two cockatiels?

2 Do birds of the same sex get along?

3 Do I have to have my landlord's permission to keep birds?

4 Is it better to buy from a breeder or a pet store?

5 Where can I get a specific color strain?

6 Are cockatiels expensive?

7 What should I watch for especially when buying a cockatiel?

8 Can cockatiels be housebroken?

9 Can cockatiels injure a person and can they represent a health hazard for humans?

10 Can cockatiels be given scraps from the table?

Cockatiels live in flocks. If you have only a little time to give full attention to the bird, you should definitely keep at least two birds.

If you don't plan to breed the birds and simply want to have them as pets, the birds' gender is immaterial. Males get along with males just as females do with females.

If you get birds simply as pets and don't keep too many, no permission is necessary.

It makes no difference, as long as either establishment is well kept and clean. But buy from someone you trust and who can advise you well.

Generally, a good pet store will be able to get you a cockatiel of the desired color, or the owner will give you the name of a serious breeder.

Compared to the price of other kinds of parrots, cockatiels are quite reasonable. Only budgerigars are cheaper. You may end up spending more on the cage and equipment than on the bird. Of course there will be ongoing expenses for food, veterinary care, and so on.

The important thing is that the bird be healthy and come from a cage where there have not been any sick birds. It is also important to get as young a bird as possible.

Not really. It is very difficult to train a cockatiel to defecate only in the cage or on its climbing tree.

Cockatiels can bite quite hard, but they use their beak as a weapon only if they feel threatened. It is very rare for them to transmit a disease to humans (see page 57).

You may occasionally give your bird fruit or bits of pasta, but feeding a cockatiel at the table regularly is harmful because of the spices in our food.

Information and advice to help you take good care of your cockatiel

The typical cockatiel: its origins, life cycle, characteristics, and more

Expert advice: selecting, feeding, health care, breeding, and caging

Appreciating your cockatiel: understanding its body language and vocal language

These exotic and colorful birds are native to Australia.

■ Step-by-step procedures on maintaining a contented, healthy bird

■ Useful addresses and references

■ Filled with handsome full-color photos

BARRON'S